D0579362

JUNIOR GEOLOGIST
Discovering Rocks, Minerals, and Gems

WHAT ARE IGNEOUS ROCKS?

ELISA PETERS

Britannica®
Educational Publishing

IN ASSOCIATION WITH

ROSEN
EDUCATIONAL SERVICES

Published in 2016 by Britannica Educational Publishing (a trademark of Encyclopædia Britannica, Inc.) in association with The Rosen Publishing Group, Inc.
29 East 21st Street, New York, NY 10010

Distributed exclusively by Rosen Publishing.
To see additional Britannica Educational Publishing titles, go to rosenpublishing.com.

First Edition

Britannica Educational Publishing
J.E. Luebering: Director, Core Reference Group
Mary Rose McCudden: Editor, Britannica Student Encyclopedia

Rosen Publishing
Jacob R. Steinberg: Editor
Nelson Sá: Art Director
Nicole Russo: Designer
Cindy Reiman: Photography Manager
Nicole Baker: Photo Researcher

Library of Congress Cataloging-in-Publication Data

Peters, Elisa, author.
  What are igneous rocks? / Elisa Peters. — First edition.
     pages cm. — (Junior geologist : discovering rocks, minerals, and gems)
  Audience: Grades 1–4.
  Includes bibliographical references and index.
  ISBN 978-1-68048-242-3 (library bound) — ISBN 978-1-5081-0047-8 (pbk.) — ISBN 978-1-68048-300-0 (6-pack)
  1. Igneous rocks—Juvenile literature. 2. Petrology—Juvenile literature. I. Title.
  QE461.P45525 2016
  552.1—dc23
                                                                                              2015016302
Manufactured in the United States of America

Photo credits: Cover, p. 1 www.sandatlas.org/Shutterstock.com; cover and interior pages background stocksolutions/Shutterstock.com; p. 4 Johnathan & Esper/Aurora/Getty Images; p. 5 © Steve Estvanik/Fotolia; p. 6 Matteo Chinellato-ChinellatoPhoto/Photographer's Choice/ Getty Images; p. 7 Kirkendall/Spring; pp. 8, 14, 16, 25 Encyclopaedia Britannica, Inc.; p. 9 Ian Graham/E+/Getty Images; p. 11 Wolfgang Kaehler/LightRocket/Getty Images; p. 12 J. D. Griggs, U.S. Geological Survey; p. 13 Emil Javorsky/EB Inc.; p. 15 Toshi Sasaki/Photographer's Choice/Getty Images; p. 17 © Merriam-Webster Inc.; pp. 18, 20 D.L Weide; p. 19 Yadid Levy/Robert Harding World Imagery/Getty Images; p. 21 Ed Freeman/Stone/Getty Images; p. 22 Pawel Toczynski/Photolibrary/Getty Images; p. 23 Nutan/Tourist Ireland; p. 24 Michael Szönyi/ imageBROKER/Getty Images; p. 26 Jon Wilson/Science Source; p. 27 Hawaii Volcano Observatory, U.S. Geological Survey; p. 28 BanksPhotos/ E+/Getty Images; p. 29 Woudloper; interior pages (arrow) Mushakesa/Shutterstock.com

CONTENTS

Made from Magma 4

A Mix of Minerals 6

The Rock Cycle 8

Magma 12

Plates and Volcanoes 16

Spotlight on Granite 20

Spotlight on Basalt 22

Volcanic Glass and Floating Rocks 24

Studying Igneous Rocks 26

Using Igneous Rocks 28

Glossary 30

For More Information 31

Index 32

MADE FROM MAGMA

Did you know that there is more than one kind of rock? Igneous rock is one of the three kinds of rock found on Earth. The other two are sedimentary rock and metamorphic rock. Each of these kinds of rock forms differently.

Igneous rock is formed from a soft, fluid substance called magma. Magma is often described as molten, or

When a volcano erupts you can see melted rock pouring out of it.

Obsidian can form sharp edges when it breaks. It was once used to make knives.

←

melted, rock. Igneous rock forms when magma cools down and hardens.

There are many types of igneous rock. Granite is one of the most common forms. This hard rock is used in building. It is also popular for kitchen countertops! Obsidian is an igneous rock, too. Obsidian is a shiny, jet-black rock. It was once used to make mirrors.

Vocabulary

When a solid is heated, it melts and becomes liquid. It is called molten when very high heat causes the melting.

A MIX OF MINERALS

As all rocks are, igneous rocks are made up of minerals. Minerals are inorganic substances. This means that they do not come from an animal or a plant. Some minerals, such as copper and silver, are metals. Sulfur, quartz, and salt are other well-known minerals.

Igneous rocks are made up of a mix of minerals. The mineral quartz is quite common in igneous rocks. So are a group of minerals known as feldspars. Igneous rocks

Quartz is the second-most common mineral in Earth's crust.

Think About It

The igneous rock diabase is dark in color. Do you think it is a mafic rock or a felsic rock?

that have a lot of feldspar and silica in them are called felsic (from feldspar and silica). They are rather light in color. Rhyolite and granite are felsic rocks. Mafic rocks have larger amounts of magnesium and iron. This makes them darker in color. Gabbro and basalt are mafic rocks.

Devils Postpile in California is made up of basalt columns that are 40 to 60 feet (12 to 18 meters) tall.

THE ROCK CYCLE

Rock is always being formed, worn down into pieces, and then formed again. This is called the rock cycle. The rock cycle takes many millions of years. As a

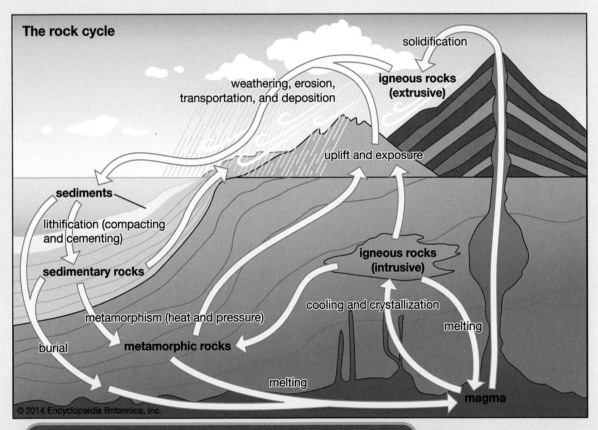

The rock cycle

solidification

weathering, erosion, transportation, and deposition

igneous rocks (extrusive)

uplift and exposure

sediments

lithification (compacting and cementing)

igneous rocks (intrusive)

sedimentary rocks

cooling and crystallization

metamorphism (heat and pressure)

melting

burial

metamorphic rocks

melting

magma

© 2014 Encyclopædia Britannica, Inc.

This diagram shows how rock can change from one type to another in the rock cycle.

result of the rock cycle, each kind of rock can become another kind of rock.

All sedimentary rocks are made up of materials that were once a part of older formations such as igneous rocks. The wind, water, and other natural forces wear rocks away and break them into ever-smaller pieces. Water washes the pieces into rivers. They settle along the river bottom in loose layers called sediment. Over millions of years the sediment builds up, hardens, and becomes solid rock.

Sedimentary rocks often form in layers, called strata.

As sediment builds up and becomes rock, it forms layers. Here you can see these layers.

This is the result of the gradual way in which layers of sediment build up.

Metamorphic rock forms from old igneous or sedimentary rock. Several forces can change old rock into new metamorphic rock. Great heat and pressure inside Earth's crust can shape old rock into metamorphic rock. Water can dissolve minerals in old rock or carry new minerals into it to form metamorphic rock. The heat of magma can also change old rock into metamorphic rock. For example, basalt can be changed into the metamorphic rock greenschist. One of the most common metamorphic rocks is gneiss (pronounced "nice"), which can form from granite under intense temperatures and pressures.

Compare and Contrast

What are the differences in the ways metamorphic and igneous rocks form? Are there any similarities?

When sedimentary rock or metamorphic rock becomes deeply buried, the heat deep within Earth may melt that rock into magma. If that magma cools down and hardens, it will become igneous rock. The rock cycle is constant, occurring again and again.

The igneous rocks in Idaho's Craters of the Moon National Monument were once magma. →

MAGMA

Magma is very hot. It exists at temperatures of 1,100° to 2,400° F (600° to 1,300° C). When it cools down, magma becomes igneous rock.

While magma is generally described as molten rock, it actually has other things mixed into it, too. The hot, liquid base of magma is called the melt. The melt has solid chunks of rock in it. It also contains dissolved gases. Minerals in the melt form crystals.

Here a flow of lava glows red hot as it moves along the ground.

Think About It

Magma that reaches Earth's surface is called lava. Why would people use a different name for the same material in different places?

Most quartz crystals, like the ones making up this rock, have six-sided columns.

→

A crystal is a certain type of solid object. All matter is made up of tiny parts called atoms and molecules. If those parts are arranged in a regular pattern then the object is a crystal. On the outside, crystals have a regular pattern of flat surfaces that meet in sharp corners. Diamonds, amethysts, and salt are all crystals.

To understand how magma forms, you need to understand Earth's structure. Earth is made up of three layers: the core, the mantle, and the crust. The core is the center of the planet. It is about 4,300 miles (6,900 kilometers) across. It is very hot. The mantle covers the core. It is about 1,800 miles (2,900 kilometers) thick. The crust is Earth's thin, rocky outer layer. At its thickest, the crust is about 19 miles (31 kilometers) thick.

mantle
1,800 miles

core
4,300 miles

crust
3–19 miles

You can see Earth's core, mantle, and crust in this diagram.

Magma forms in the lower part of the crust and the upper part of the mantle. It forms in spots where the temperature is very hot. It also forms in places where the pressure between the layers decreases. The presence of water and the gas carbon dioxide can also cause magma to form. They lower the melting point for rock.

Magma escapes through the crust as lava during an eruption in Hawaii.

Vocabulary

The melting point is the temperature at which a solid becomes a liquid.

PLATES AND VOLCANOES

Earth's crust is made up of large pieces of solid rock called plates. The plates move around on the partially melted rock that lies below them. Magma often forms at places where the plates push against, under, or past each other. Magma also forms at thin spots in the crust.

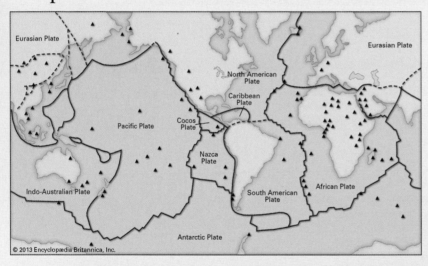

Because magma is less dense than the surrounding solid rocks, it rises toward the surface. It may settle within the crust or erupt

This diagram shows the main tectonic plates that make up Earth's crust.

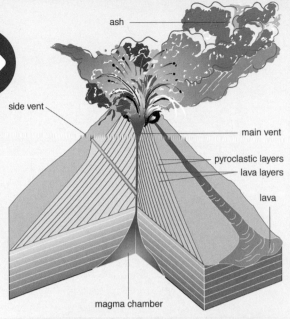

ash

side vent

main vent

pyroclastic layers

lava layers

lava

magma chamber

at the surface from a volcano. When a volcano erupts, hot gases and magma from deep within Earth find their way up to the surface. This material may flow slowly out of a crack in the ground. It can also explode suddenly into the air. Volcanic eruptions may be very destructive. However, they also create new landforms.

Some igneous rocks are intrusive while others are extrusive. Intrusive rock forms when magma cools slowly, usually deep underground. As the molten rock cools, the minerals in it form fairly large crystals. Intrusive rocks often look speckled, or made

Vocabulary

A volcano is a vent in Earth's crust from which melted or hot rock and steam come out.

17

Granite is an intrusive rock that forms deep within Earth's crust. It is rich in quartz and feldspar.

up of many small patches of color. Granite, diorite, and gabbro are all intrusive igneous rocks.

Extrusive igneous rock forms when magma cools quickly, usually because it comes to the surface of Earth.

Think About It

Diorite and andesite have a similar mix of minerals. Diorite is speckled white and black. Andesite is an uneven gray. Which one is the extrusive rock?

You can't see the individual grains in fine-grained rocks such as basalt. These basalt cliffs are in Iceland.

It generally cools too quickly for large crystals to form. Extrusive rocks, such as basalt, are fine-grained.

Magma with the same mix of minerals in it will form different rocks depending on how quickly it cools. For example, magma that would form gabbro if it cools slowly will form basalt if it cools quickly.

SPOTLIGHT ON GRANITE

Granite is the most common igneous rock in Earth's crust. Looking at a piece of granite, one can easily pick out the minerals that make it up. One such mineral is quartz. The particles often look like smoky glass. Granite also has a lot of feldspar. Mica, whose thin, flat particles reflect

This close-up view of the mineral grains in quartz is magnified one and a half times.

Vocabulary

Particles are very small pieces of something.

light like tiny mirrors, is also present.

The color of granite depends on the amounts and the kinds of minerals in it. The most common color is gray. It is dark gray if it contains many dark minerals and light if they are few. Green, pink, and blue colors are due to different kinds of feldspar.

Granite is common in nature. California's beautiful Sierra Nevada mountains are mostly made of granite. New Hampshire's nickname is the Granite State, from its many granite quarries.

California's Mount Whitney is made mostly of granite.

SPOTLIGHT ON BASALT

Basalt is the most common extrusive rock on Earth. It is dark gray or black in color. Basalt is denser than most other extrusive rocks. It contains less silica and more iron and magnesia than the other common extrusive rocks, such as rhyolite. Its chief minerals are feldspar, pyroxene, olivine, and iron oxides. Because of its density and toughness, basalt is often used for making roads and buildings.

Basalt is found throughout the world. Most of the lava that pours out

These dark basalt rocks are along the north shore of the Hawaiian island of Oahu.

Ireland's Giant's Causeway is made up of about 40,000 basalt columns.

of volcanoes that make up oceanic islands is basaltic. For example, Hawaii's Mauna Loa is made up of basaltic lava flows.

Think About It

Most of the crust under Earth's oceans is made of basalt. Why do you think this is?

Where flows of liquid lava cool down slowly and evenly, the newly hardened material shrinks and cracks into columns with several sides. Well-known examples of these columns can be seen at the Giant's Causeway in Ireland.

VOLCANIC GLASS AND FLOATING ROCKS

Rhyolite lava has a lot of silica in it. This makes it lighter in weight and color than the lava that hardens into basalt. Rhyolite lava is very thick. This means that it flows slowly. When this kind of lava cools rapidly, it may form a dark natural glass called obsidian. In the past, people made tools such as arrowheads from obsidian. Obsidian is still used to make jewelry.

Pumice is another unusual igneous rock. This

This obsidian boulder is from Lava Beds National Monument in California. →

lightweight stone forms from lava that is full of small, tightly packed gas bubbles. Pumice is so light that it can float in water! People use pumice stones to rub off dry skin, especially on their feet! It is also used to make lightweight concrete.

Vocabulary

Concrete is a hard, strong building material made by mixing cement, sand, and gravel or broken rock with water.

This hardened lava was converted into layers of pumice and obsidian by escaping gases.

STUDYING IGNEOUS ROCKS

This petrologist is studying a series of rock samples under a microscope.

Scientists who study the physical features and history of Earth are called geologists. Several kinds of geologists study igneous rocks. Petrology is the study of the history and structure of rocks, particularly igneous and metamorphic rocks. Petrologists (those who study petrology) study where different rocks are found and how rocks form. They help us understand how Earth got its present shape and form.

Compare and Contrast

How do you think petrology and volcanology are similar? In what ways are their focuses different?

Volcanology is the branch of geology that focuses on volcanoes. Many volcanologists work in observatories. This is where they keep track of earth tremors and other signs of volcanic activity. Others venture forth to the slopes and craters for an even closer look. On the basis of what they measure and see, they try to predict volcanic activity. They predict when an eruption might take place, how severe it will be, and which places will be in the danger zone.

This geologist is gathering lava samples on Kilauea, a volcano in Hawaii.

USING IGNEOUS ROCKS

Concrete often contains igneous rock. This batch of concrete will be used to pave a sidewalk.

People have found many ways to use igneous rocks. The rocks are used to make gravel and concrete. They are also used in road construction. Hard, long-lasting granite shines when it is polished. It is often used for tombstones and monuments. Some sculptures, such as Mount Rushmore, are made of granite. Basalt is one of the rocks used as track ballast on railroads. Ballast is the crushed rock underneath train tracks. It supports the railroad ties and rails.

Igneous rocks can contain buried treasure. The intrusive igneous rock kimberlite is one of the main sources of diamonds. Such valuable metals as gold, nickel, lead, zinc, iron, and copper are all found in igneous rocks. These are taken from the earth by mining.

Kimberlite is named after Kimberley, South Africa, where it was found in large deposits.

GLOSSARY

dense Made of atoms packed tightly together.

dissolve To mix completely into a liquid.

erupt To burst forth or cause to burst forth.

extrusive rock Igneous rock that forms quickly on Earth's surface.

felsic Containing large amounts of silica and feldspar.

fine-grained Made up of very small parts or grains.

fluid Moving and flowing easily.

gases Matter in which atoms are not in a fixed shape and will flow to fill a space. Air is a gas.

intrusive rock Igneous rock that forms slowly, deep inside Earth.

lava Melted rock that flows from a volcano or other opening in the surface of Earth.

liquid Matter in which atoms are not in a fixed shape but will take the shape of a container. Water is a liquid.

mafic Containing high amounts of magnesium and iron.

magma Molten rock material within Earth.

metamorphic rock Rock that is changed into another form by the action of pressure, heat, and water.

observatories Places equipped with instruments for the observation of natural objects and events.

oceanic Having to do with an ocean.

pressure The application of force to an object by something else in direct contact with it.

quarries Open pits from which people take stone for building or other uses.

sedimentary rock Rock that forms from sediment, or small bits of older rock that build up over time.

solid Matter in which atoms hold in a fixed shape. Wood and rocks are solids.

FOR MORE INFORMATION

BOOKS

Aloian, Molly. *What Are Igneous Rocks?* (Let's Rock!). New York, NY: Crabtree Publishing Company, 2010.

Brown, Cynthia Light, and Nick Brown. *Explore Rocks and Minerals!: 25 Great Projects, Activities, Experiments* (Explore Your World). White River Junction, VT: Nomad Press, 2010.

Dee, Willa. *Unearthing Igneous Rocks* (Rocks: The Hard Facts). New York, NY: PowerKids Press, 2014.

Lawrence, Ellen. *How Do Volcanoes Make Rock? A Look at Igneous Rock* (Rock-Ology). New York, NY: Bearport Publishing, 2014.

Nelson, Maria. *Igneous Rocks* (That Rocks!). New York, NY: Gareth Stevens Publishing, 2011.

Owings, Lisa. *Igneous Rocks* (Rocks and Minerals). Edina, MN: ABDO, 2015.

WEBSITES

Because of the changing nature of Internet links, Rosen Publishing has developed an online list of websites related to the subject of this book. This site is updated regularly. Please use this link to access the list:

http://www.rosenlinks.com/GEOL/Ign

INDEX

basalt, 7, 10, 19, 22–23, 28

crust, Earth's, 10, 14–15, 16, 20
crystals, 12–14, 17, 19

feldspar, 6–7, 20, 21, 22
felsic rocks, 7

granite, 5, 7, 10, 18, 20–21, 28, 29

igneous rock
    extrusive, 17, 18–19, 22
    formation of, 4–5, 11
    intrusive, 17–18, 29

studying, 26–27
using, 28–29
iron, 7, 22, 29

lava, 13, 22–23, 24, 25

mafic rocks, 7
magma, 4–5, 10, 11, 12–15, 16–17, 18, 19
mantle, Earth's, 14–15
metamorphic rock, 4, 10, 11, 26
minerals, 6–7, 17, 18, 19, 20–21
molten rock, 4–5, 12, 17

petrologists, 26
plates, 16
pumice, 24–25

quartz, 6, 20

rock cycle, 8–11

sedimentary rock, 4, 9–10, 11

volcanoes, 17, 23, 24–25, 27
volcanologists, 27